Manny's New Friend

Alexis McDonald
Artwork by Mary Judge

AuthorHouse™ LLC
1663 Liberty Drive
Bloomington, IN 47403
www.authorhouse.com
Phone: 1-800-839-8640

Published by AuthorHouse 04/16/2014

ISBN: 978-1-4969-0303-7 (sc)
ISBN: 978-1-4969-0304-4 (e)

authorHOUSE®

My Mom's been tired and I don't know why.
Is she coming down with the flu?
She even seems like she may cry.

There are more visitors than normal. Is something going on?
Are we having a party? Never mind they're all gone.

Tilly's one of my friends.
She really likes to nap.
She usually likes to be by herself,
but now Tilly's on Mom's lap.

Mom has this new thing she pushes on our walks.

It's big and rolls next to me.

When I smell it and look back at her, she says

"I can't wait for everyone to see."

Mom goes to the barn to visit Karma.
She's usually gone for a while.
She used to ride her every visit,
but now she doesn't go in style.

There's been a change in one of the rooms.
It's full of new furniture and toys.

It's full of new smells and I don't know why.
A lot of the toys make noise.

Mom and Dad are taking me to the hotel.
I know from the road bend.
Mom kisses me on the head and says
"soon you get to meet your new friend."

I have a visitor when I'm there.
She's a great friend and I know her well.
She brings me a gift from Mom and Dad.
I know it's from them from the smell.

It also smells of someone new, but I don't know who it is.
Is this the friend that Mom talked about?
I think this blanket is his.

Dad picks me up from the hotel and plays with me in the yard.
When we go inside and up to the room he seems very on guard.

Mom's in bed. I'm so happy to see her
but she just doesn't get up.
She smiles and pets me on the head.
Is she holding a new pup?

He's not a pup! He's a baby boy and he belongs to my Mom and Dad.

I want to meet him and kiss him and smell him. Does he smell good or bad?

My friend Max knows about our new friend.
He's seen the baby boy, too.

The baby makes little noises.
He squeaks and cries and also goes "Coo."

I love my new friend, though he doesn't do much.
He lies around like a log.

My Mom says we will grow up to be best friends
because I'm the best dog.

Printed in the United States
by Baker & Taylor Publisher Services